BEAT THE STATISTICS

THE 9 SKILLS TO ENSURE YOU SURVIVE AND THRIVE IN BUSINESS

By Martin Sharp

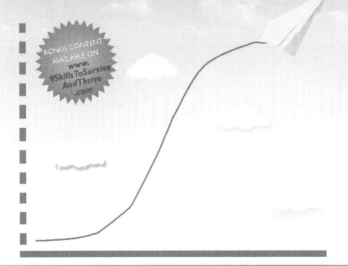

FOREWORD BY SUNDAY TIMES
BEST SELLING AUTHOR ANDY HARRINGTON

BEAT THE STATISTICS

THE 9 SKILLS TO ENSURE YOU SURVIVE AND THRIVE IN BUSINESS

BONUS CONTENT
AVAILABLE ON
www.
9SkillsToSurvive
AndThrive
.com

MARTIN SHARP

BEAT THE STATISTICS

THE 9 SKILLS TO ENSURE YOU SURVIVE AND THRIVE IN
BUSINESS

Published by Waxtie Ltd
211 Viking House, 13 Micklegate, York, YO1 6RA
First Published in 2019

For information about special discounts for bulk purchases, please
contact Waxtie Ltd +44 1904 293270

ISBN: 978-1-0865-3309-5

DEDICATION

*For my 25 year old self - what I wish
I'd known at the start. For all those
I've helped since starting and those
that have helped me, thank you for
sharing the journey.*

Martin Sharp

TESTIMONIAL

"Great session with Martin Sharp, I am really making progress here on subjects that need to work perfectly and smoothly. Thank you!"

Colin Luthardt - Director of Seco

"I spoke on the big stage of Retail Expo, London Olympia in front of 100 people, including standing up for the late arrivals. 80% of the audience did my Call to Action and 20% of them followed up with the additional action. Massive thanks to Martin Sharp for all your inputs, inspiration and support! You are simply amazing"

Bilyana Georgieva - Business Transformation Expert

CONTENTS

ACKNOWLEDGEMENTS

I have to start by thanking my awesome wife and co-director, Sarah. For encouraging me every day, reading the drafts, being a sounding board of the themes and editor. Let alone the million and one other things you do for our family and me. I am truly blessed and thank you so much.

Having an idea and turning it into a book is as hard as it sounds. Thank you to Helen, who has helped me so much in the development of this book and its ideas. Who has reviewed the book and suggested ways to make it even better and developed the associated web pages to make it an even greater resource for you.

Without the experience and dedication of John Oddy and Mark Overend, who tirelessly ensure we stay on the right path and offer options and answers when I don't have any, along with being brilliant accountants, I'm sure we would have ended as a statistic ourselves. A great testimony that you don't need to have all the answers, yet you do need to surround yourself with people who do.

To Asad Ali, a genuinely helpful person and a great source of legal advice when things are going well or not so well. Hopefully, you know how comforting it is to know you are there when needed.

There are three circles of people in your life. Those whom you serve and become your clients. Those whom you learn and have a laugh with, who are your peers. And those whom you learn from, who've trodden the path before you and can steer you away from the traps. The mentors in your life, those you look up to and want to imitate. I'd especially like to thank two of my mentors: Andrew Mason for kick-starting my entrepreneurial adventure and helping me to learn what it is to be a business owner. And Andy Harrington, who alongside improving my speaking skills, also provided insights into how to improve the entire front end of my business.

There are also times when you need some accountability to keep you in action, so you don't slide into spinning the wheels and you keep pushing yourself forward. So, I'd like to give a special thanks to James Dewane, Cheryl Chapman, Michelle Watson, Deenita Pattni, Marion Bevington, Carole Fossey and Vish Babber for holding me to account, holding me to a higher standard and encouraging me to go and grow where others won't. I've learned a lot, laughed a lot and had a great time doing it.

FOREWORD

Firstly, a massive congratulations to Martin Sharp on completing over 10 years in owning his businesses and over 20 years of delivering successful transformational change in other peoples' companies. As we know, it is definitely not easy to maintain a business for a considerable period of time, and he is definitely bucking the trend, as most businesses simply don't make it and his are thriving.

The reason they are thriving is that he is an excellent consultant with insightful use of his knowledge, know-how and experience, that he passes on to others.

He really is a master of his craft, and I'm so thrilled and delighted that he's also chosen to be a part of my business as one of my Accredited Coaching Executives, mentoring my clients, who are now achieving their own successes. For me, the feedback that he gives people is always right on the money and most importantly delivered in a style that makes it easily digestible to be absorbed by other people. He truly is a talent, and I realise and know just how important a part of my organisation he is.

Maybe you picked up this book in a bookstore or library? Or perhaps you bought it on Amazon or received it as a gift? However, you came to have hold of this book, you have one of life's little gems. Because here's the thing, it is not every day that someone with this level of experience shares with you how to be a success.

Within these pages, Martin has set out, in his customary down to earth fashion, the 9 skills that I, along with many other successful small business owners, have had to learn and master over the years to have thriving businesses. Many lessons though I acquired through trial and terror, whereas by reading this, you will already have a head start.

This book is a fantastic resource if you already have a business and are looking at what it takes to grow, ensure profitability and make sure it keeps coming. Or if you are just setting out in business or even if you are considering setting up a business wondering what skills you will need.

I'm sure that by taking action and thoroughly answering the thought-provoking questions presented, you'll be starting on your way to what I've found to be one of the greatest missions of my life, running a successful business that helps others and supports my family and me. Like Martin says, "to get a good answer, you have to ask a good question."

So, again huge thanks to Martin and his team. A massive kudos for your 10 years in business and the clients that they work with have who will continue to indeed become great themselves.

I wish you all the health, wealth and happiness.

Andy Harrington - Sunday Times Best Selling Author – CEO Jet Set Speaker Ltd

YOU HAVE A TOUGH DECISION

CAN YOU MAKE IT?

It's October 2012, and I am sitting behind my oak coloured Ikea desk, staring blankly at the screen of my silver HP 15" ProBook laptop. There in front of me is my cashflow forecast and profit & loss projection, both showing the time to death of my business in 2 months!

All this came about because I helped a client by accelerating a piece of work through without all the necessary paperwork, circumventing my processes and now I don't have enough funds available to survive.

I've already sunk in all my capital, that of friends and family and the bank is not willing to extend any credit.

What would you do?

Maybe you have or will experience a decision point in your business, that make or break moment when your business can survive and thrive, or collapse to become another statistic. Potentially this is one of those things that keep you awake at night or stops you from taking advantage of all those opportunities that present themselves.

Perhaps you are reading this because you want to make money from your business? Not only make money though, but you'd also like to be able to do this year in, year out. Yet you are currently yoyo-ing from feast to famine, not knowing how you will pay your mortgage from month to month, which inevitably makes you stressed, frustrated and feeling like giving up.

You are possibly searching for more information on how best to run a business, as you may never have owned or run one before? Perhaps you are looking at how to run a business better than you have done before because you don't want to make silly mistakes that can be avoided?

If this sounds like you, then what if you had the skills and knowledge to be able to recognise a potential problem in your business before it causes you trouble? Then you could take the necessary corrective action and even benefit from the opportunities that the resolution uncovers?

Imagine that your business is running like a well-oiled machine. You can predict your income before it happens and people around you are ensuring it materialises so that you don't have to do everything yourself.

Picture the scenario, the day when people in your organisation are seeking you out for answers, and you know exactly what to say? You have the skills, the know-how and the confidence to know what direction to go in.

If you are currently facing problems within your business, yet want to be a business owner with answers and direction, then do you agree something needs to change?

Great because that is what you are going to read about in this book. Specifically, what skills does it take to make your business survive and thrive?

Now, what do I mean by survive and thrive? I mean simply moving beyond the situation that you may be in right now and into a position where your business will flourish, grow and develop for you, and those within your ecosystem will also prosper from that success.

For this to happen, it takes skills, ingenuity, creativity and drive:

Skills in being able to run your own business, as described in many business books. Personally, I like the way Michael Gerber in E-Myth Revisited describes that moment of the "Entrepreneurial Seizure". That is the moment when you realise that you have the skills to create something amazing because your "do" is better than everyone else's "do". Consequently, you setup your own business, which you may or may not have had any training or have any skills in running!

Ingenious and resourceful is about being able to find win-win answers to any problems and struggles you encounter so that you can relieve your client of their problems and be able to profit from it.

Creative relates to being able to solve problems. After all, the only reason why any business exists is that there is a problem that someone else has and they will pay money for you to solve it. This also includes products and luxury goods. The 'problem' people have relating to products, is that they can't make whatever it is themselves.

Drive, passion, spirit, choose the word that most resonates with you that means you have the fire to continue even when worn out, when the problems are mounting or even when it seems like there is no solution. This will drive you through the blockers, power over the obstacles and will carry you to the success that lies just beyond the failure.

Don't just take my word for it, in 2018 an 8-year study by leading UK Universities and Goldman Sachs* found...

Small business IS the backbone of UK economy representing:

✓ 99% of businesses, 5.6m businesses in the UK
✓ 99% of UK employer firms
✓ 51% of UK revenue
✓ Employ over 60% or 16m of the UK workforce

Small Businesses who have the training and mentoring grow 16x faster, achieve 25% faster revenue growth and require 23% more people than comparable businesses in the same sector. They do this through changed behaviour and improved strategy, which results in:

✓ 28% high productivity
✓ 74% increase in training
✓ 71% grow with finance
✓ 62% new product or service
✓ 97% more effective leaders
✓ 94% more confident

✓ 90% implement new business processes
✓ 84% use financial data

What is the Small Business Failure Rate you may be wondering?

The UK Government Office for National Statistics publishes a report on the Business births, deaths and survival rates each year. When looking over this year on year, a pattern emerges that is well quoted. That is, "10% don't make it to their first birthday, 35% fail before their second anniversary, and 50% are no longer trading before their third."

With only 10% surviving to celebrate 10 years in business, some people wonder why you should bother?

While the savvier of you are thinking, how do I get to know what the 10% know to be successful?

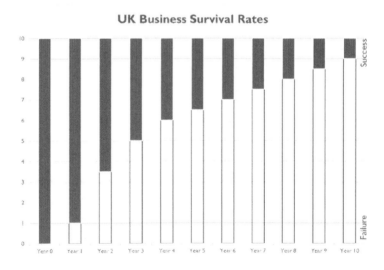

UK Business Survival Rates

The good news is that if you are still in business or

thinking about setting up in business, then you are still in the game and should congratulate yourselves in making it this far. You can make it to 10 years and beyond, what's stopping you?

With a minefield of potential disasters out there, it would be fair to say that any business, large or small, is only six months away from failure given the right conditions. Business Insurance firm Hiscox Inc, conducted a study into what were the most common reasons for failure in UK businesses and their findings included:

"Businesses ran out of money." "Cash is king", you hear every business guru say and for a good reason. Money is the lifeblood of your organisation. Just like blood in the human body, without money, your business cannot survive. You cannot pay its bills, you cannot pay any staff, and as such, you cannot fulfil your orders or obligations to your clients, regulators or government. It goes without saying that it is vital that any business, especially a small business, has a plan for how they will get paid, and importantly in a timely manner. Even the most successful businesses can find themselves in trouble if their money is all tied up in unpaid invoices.

"Fail to plan, plan to fail" is another battle cry repeated like a bad cliché.

The thing is most leaders agree that it is always good to have a plan, just like a map for finding your way. Not just for getting to your destination, the map is also there to show you when you are off track or help you find a detour past that hazard. Your business should have a plan of what you will achieve and how you will achieve it in the next 12 months, written out and clearly communicated to all the important players inside the business and supporting your business.

"Me 2" or you look no different from the competition and have a lack of a clear value proposition, whether that is a unique selling proposition or an extra value proposition. If you aren't clear on how you're different or better than the competition, how can you expect your customers to see you as any different?

"Being too dependent on one or two big customers" is all too often where small businesses become complacent, relying on them too heavily. Whether that is because they don't believe they have the bandwidth to service more smaller customers, or don't have a repeatable model, or simply because they stopped marketing when they were happy just serving the customers they have, perpetuating the feast and famine scenario. This can be exacerbated if one of those big customers goes away.

"Only a website" is not marketing! There are many small businesses that believe that opening their doors, hanging out a sign, putting up a website or some other minor act is enough to make customers appear. The thing is it rarely works that way, and you need to have a clear marketing platform and plan always to be marketing yourself.

"Where are we?" Every business needs to have key performance indicators that let it know where it is against the plan. Yet we still hear so many small business owners or managers exclaim that "My company isn't big enough to need performance data, I just talk to people.". The problem is they are wrong! Every business, at every level, can collect and analyse performance data, these days –

whether it's the conversion rate of your website or counting the number of people who only enter your shop compared to those who pass by. How do you know where you are on your plan unless you measure it? If it isn't measured, it isn't managed!

"Too much working in the business and not enough working on the business." Poor leadership and management because the business owner cannot let go of the day-to-day minutiae of running their businesses can be the death knell announcing another business failed. If you find yourself focused on ordering printer supplies and cleaning out the office refrigerator, then you can be sure that you are not focused on the more important tasks.

"Not listening to your customers" in regard to what they want, is a sure-fire way of "losing friends and alienating people." As a business owner if you believe you know what's best for your customers, but you are not collecting information from them and the market to know what they are actually saying, then you are setting yourself up for failure.

"No data security or backup!" If you've ever had a computer fail or lost your smartphone, you will understand how catastrophic it can be and how disruptive to your life. Now, imagine losing all of your data for your business. Now try to imagine the chaos if your customer data were to be hacked or stolen. It could easily end your business.

If you have the drive, creativity and ingenuity, would you agree that now is the best time to get the skills you need to be able to run a surviving and thriving business?

And if not now when?

Now back in October 2012, 3 years in from setting up my business in July 2009, I had one of those decision points. One of many that would come up in my business, testing the business and myself as the leader.

How did I survive, you may be wondering? Well, let me introduce you to John Oddy, my accountant, who looks a little bit like Chris Hemsworth. Whereas most typical accountants talk to you about tax planning, budgeting, book-keeping and a plethora of things that would send the most chronic insomniac into the land of slumber, John didn't do that. Now don't get me wrong, he has an army of people in his firm that he can call on for such an occasion, so the mechanics of accounts get done.

Ever since setting up John has been my business mentor keeping me on the right path, while at the same time giving me the choice of how I run my business by providing three answers to every question:

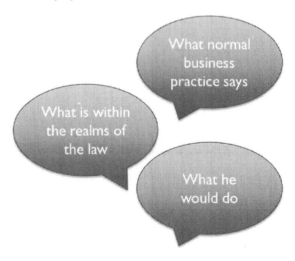

"John, the client hasn't paid their invoice. I've chased for over 60 days now only to be told that because we worked above and beyond what was contractually agreed, even though they verbally agreed to it, they won't pay unless I change the invoice to the contractual amount. I spoke to my solicitor, and the only option remaining is to take them to small claims court, which will take more money. And even if I'm awarded, there is no guarantee they will pay! What am I to do?"

"You need to improve your cashflow Martin so you can get over this."

"Really!! That's obvious!!" I thought, although didn't voice it. "Do you have any suggestions, John?"

"Sure Martin, you can raise some more sales with shorter payment terms or even better payment upfront. Or you need to cut your costs, which may mean reducing the number of clients you serve and the amount of work you do."

Sounds simple, doesn't it? It was great that we had a plan and KPI's in place to have spotted this early. Yet still, the options weren't great. Therefore, within a few days of that conversation, I gathered together the team for an all-hands brainstorming session in a meeting room at the Mercure Hotel.

It was a poorly lit room due to a tree growing in front of the window and smelled of stale coffee. With a heavy heart I laid out before them all that had happened, which wasn't a surprise as I'd kept them informed throughout.

"I'm looking for other ideas as I've only come up with

three options: One - we all pull together and try to bring in more sales. Two - we accept pay cuts and weather the storm returning to normal after. Or three, we have to consider some redundancies." The words felt like fishbones in my throat.

Some of the team opted for redundancies, while the rest pushed forwards. Winning more work, delivering transformative changes in business environments, improving profitability for our clients and our business, while delivering great service.

And the reasons the business got through this wasn't because I was something special, it was all down to having the right skills, the drive, creativity and ingenuity to make it a success.

So, what are the 9 Skills to Ensure you survive and thrive in your first 5 years, you may be wondering?

And I'm a busy person so will this benefit me?

Visit the book page for bonus content on

www.9skillstosurviveandthrive.com

IS THIS FOR ME?

Let me tell you who this book is written for. It is written for entrepreneurial people, business owners, managers or consultants who want to reach more people, further improve their business or those seeking to increase their skillset. Whether they are currently in business, seeking to set up a business or run someone else's business.

It is for those who want to specialise in a niche area in business, rather than getting lost trying to do everything for everyone.

Whether they want to work with corporates, other small businesses or work with the general public, it's for people who want to help people overcome a challenge in their personal lives. It's for people who want to help customers in sales or marketing. For operations, delivery or fulfilment. For business services or support.

It's for you if success, quality service and profit is what you strive for. If you have passion, drive, energy and focus, yet are humble enough to learn from those who went before. After all, a knowledgeable person learns from their mistakes, a wise person learns from the mistakes of others and the foolish person repeats their mistakes.

If you are the former, then within these pages, you'll find 9 key skill areas to work on that have helped me build my businesses and assist in transforming the businesses of others.

However, this is not for you if you are happy where you are right now and have no desire to change anything.

If you feel you are already serving your clients and your

organisation at the highest level and don't want or need to improve anything.

And you believe you have the right measures, systems and processes in place and don't need to change anything.

Or if you believe that you have all the skills you need and don't need to learn anything new.

Then this is not for you.

This is for you if you want to be incredible and outstanding and build a business that can make you hundreds of thousands, if not millions. By doing what you do best - helping to solve the problems of your clients and delivering the great service. People with dreams and aspirations, people with an overriding mission and vision for what they want to do with their lives.

It's for you if you recognise you are in the right place at the right time. If you want to leverage the information age, rather than wait to be a statistic.

While what you will read in this book is not a, "how-to guide", it will give clear pointers into what skills to concentrate on to improve yourself and your business. For this to happen, you need to take action.

If you don't take action, and you simply only consume this information and never implement the ideas, then nothing will change from where you are now. Perhaps you won't take any notes, create any follow up tasks or research and improve each skill. If so, the results will be elusive.

Whereas, if you know that to get results from this

information you will need to be ready to take notes, ready to ask questions, ready to research, as you arrive with the intent to implement what you learn. Well then – results will follow.

My results are not typical, and your results will vary from mine depending on the action you take!

So, you've read about one of my experiences as an entrepreneur and business owner.. Now let's look at you, and how you can become the business owner, you aspire to be.

I've discovered there are just nine skills that you need to master to have a surviving and thriving business.

"Action speaks louder than words but not nearly as often."

— *Mark Twain*

THE FOUNDATIONAL FOUR

Regardless of your business size, the Foundational Four skills are essential in being able to run a growing, profitable and sustainable business. Without these skills, it could be argued that you don't have a business, you have an idea with potential.

The first of these can be easily overlooked if your business is already operating and especially if it has been doing so for a while. Yet when you have clarity over this, and it is written down for you and your team to refer to, it can be one of the most powerful, directive and motivational items at your disposal.

What this is to have a clear **Concept**. Now, what do I mean by Concept? The concept is the understanding of what your business does, why it does it, and who it does it for.

At the same time, it is all about you, because in the beginning you and the business are one and the same. While some people believe you give birth to a business and nurture it like a child watching it grow. I don't believe this goes far enough to explain the relationship.

When a business does well, its owner does well. When a business has ill health and stress, you are likely to find a business owner suffering the same symptoms. Therefore, you can think of it in the early years, probably until you exit, like a conjoined twin. That being the case, you have to have a clear understanding of what and why YOU are doing this? What will YOU get from it? And what sacrifices are YOU willing to make to make it work?

Some business owners believe that they don't need to

write any of these answers down, because they know them and tell people about them when they join their business. I hear excuses like "I don't know what to write", "who else will read it", "it is a waste of time as my business evolves", "it's all in my head where it is safe" and "this doesn't make any sense to me, I just want to get on with bringing money in".

I believe this is fundamentally flawed and leads to several failures.

For a start, while you may know your business concept, telling someone you employ about it only when they start, means it is likely that they will forget over time. This will lead to them taking actions or making decisions that may not be in line with the business. Not because they are doing so maliciously, but because they don't recognise, they are not aligned with the strategy.

If you have ever worked in corporate business, this is something you will recognise in a highly amplified way as the message gets diluted the further away from the senior leadership team you go.

Not only that, as a business owner yourself, you may find that you end up with "shiny object syndrome". By which I mean, you are so caught up in survival mode and trying to bring money into the business that you chase after any and every piece of work. And you pursue it regardless of whether you have the right skills or whether it is aligned with what you are delivering. This behaviour is distracting and magnifies the feast and famine problem further.

Yet with a clear set of guiding principles and an

understanding of what you do, why you do it and who you do it for, you have a measure by which to grade each opportunity. You will have criteria for evaluating each marketing campaign. And most importantly, you will have a reminder when things feel at their worst, of why it is that you get up every morning.

It's a bit like looking for a new home. If you are like me, then you probably have a list of criteria that the new place needs to fulfil. This might be location - are you a city dweller or do you long for the peace of the countryside? Do you need local amenities, a train station to commute, a local shop or park to stroll? Perhaps you have kids so the quality of the schools nearby, their catchment areas and what children's facilities become a concern.

How much space do you need? Just a small space for you? Perhaps a spare room for the family or friends to stay over? Maybe you want a workshop area, or you work from home, so an office space is essential?

The point is that you have a series of criteria that you can measure each upcoming property against. And at some point, you will have to shortlist all those properties which are available and potentially you may have to compromise due to the price or perhaps you cannot get all that you want in that specific location.

With the list of criteria, you have created, you can easily prioritise which are the most important and be more confident that you haven't forgotten something. Without the list, you'll be relying on your memory (or the memory of those deciding with you) to ensure you don't forget something. Or you may end up going on purely kerb appeal and find that living there is a nightmare as it doesn't have enough space, amenities, transport, etc. that you required.

This is the same as not having a clear written understanding of your business Concept. The opportunity to paint a bedroom for £200 may be great if you are a decorator but less good if you are an accountant.

While this is an extreme example to illustrate a point, how many times have you been in a situation where a client or customer has asked: "can you just...." And they insert a request outside your expertise or normal supply? A request that may require you to take extra time to source, or time to skill up or use capital to invest in equipment. Do you know that the investment is well spent and aligned to your business Concept or should you be recommending someone else fulfils the work?

ACTION: Will you challenge yourself to start writing down your business concept and sharing it with those in your business?

The concept of my business is... ✍

...continued...✍

You may have heard the saying that "A problem shared, is a problem halved". I believe it also works with ideas.

"An idea correctly shared, is an opportunity multiplied."

— Martin Sharp

What I have found is that many people fear this skill when they start out, because they are unsure of what is needed or don't have the right people to help them. Yet when the fear is embraced, the knowledge is learnt and the stability and growth can be predicted, it is almost like having your own crystal ball. This is the skill of **Control**. Specifically, this is the skill of financial control of your business.

Like it or not, money is the lifeblood of your organisation, and it is the universal measure that is applied to all businesses, initiatives and changes. Therefore, taking control over your business (and personal) finances must be high on your list of priorities.

I've come across business owners and managers that believe by having an accountant they have financial control, therefore don't have to worry about it anymore.

For me, this is a very poor attitude to take, as it is effectively abdicating your responsibility for the financial stability or growth of your business or department to someone else. This puts them in control rather than you. Certainly, you should use skilled accountants, financial controllers, bookkeepers, tax advisors and other professionals to take care of the minutia, because your time is better spent elsewhere. However, having a good understanding of the 3 financial statements that tell the story of your business, and the selection and monitoring of the correct Key Performance Indicators (KPIs) should be considered basic knowledge.

Along with the ability to forecast the financial future for your business has to be a set of skills you acquire and continue to hone throughout your career. Because the more you practice, monitor and adjust with feedback (failures), the better you become at forecasting more accurately for the particulars of your own business and industry.

Worse still, I've come across businesses where they will avoid speaking to the accountant or accounts team because they feel confused by the jargon and worry about looking stupid or asking questions because they won't understand the answer.

For me though, the accountant and accounts team are like your wingmen ready to tell you when trouble is coming and guiding you on the right path to avoid it. You need to understand that there are no stupid questions, only the one you didn't ask. And if you don't understand something, you can always ask for it to be explained. After all, communication is a two-way process, right? And the other person has a responsibility to be able to convey a message in an understandable way or you'd be wise to seek an alternative provider.

"If you can't explain it simply, you don't understand it well enough." –
Albert Einstein

Then there are some people who believe they should do everything themselves or don't trust other people with their business finances.

Doing everything themselves is simply putting a glass

ceiling on your growth because you only have so many hours in the day. And if you are chasing payments, paying suppliers, reconciling bank accounts, preparing reports and the variety of other activities you need to run a business, then you are not doing the other things that need your attention. And that is leading your business, bringing in new clients, nurturing the relationships with existing clients and vendors, and working on your business.

Think about it a bit like learning to drive. When you first started you probably didn't know what all the controls were, you "bunny hopped" down the road trying to control the accelerator, clutch and gears and hadn't developed a good enough road sense to predict what other road users may do.

These skills were probably still in development as you passed your test and it is not until years and many, many driving miles/hours of practice that it becomes second nature. You have muscle memory about depressing the clutch while releasing the accelerator and moving the gear stick to select the next one, which results in a smooth(er) transition of power.

You know what all the controls are and rarely reach for the indicators only to put the windscreen wipers on instead. Yep we've all done it, let alone the times when you are driving abroad with the controls on the opposite side, with kids playing the game "how many times will dad try to change gear with the wing mirror!" And today, I bet you don't panic as much when a driver starts to slow down in front of you or you come to a junction as you used to when you first got behind the wheel of a car.

Running your business is the same. At the start, a

balance sheet is an enigma, Profit and loss potentially a nightmare and cashflow is accidental. Let alone forecasting beyond dreams or wishful thinking or understanding how to raise capital.

Yet by hiring the right people, spending time to understand these aspects of running your business along with asking lots of questions, like driving a car - you develop your own ability and skill. And by doing this in your own business, it is tailored specifically to how your business works, how your clients operate and the nuances of your industry and is not a theoretical model.

ACTION: Will you take the time to understand your business story through its 3 financial statements? Will you choose your advisors wisely and seek knowledge by asking lots of questions? Do you have a great accountant, solicitor and business mentor? Or will you run your business blindly and fear that end of year meeting when you have to submit your taxes and hope you've not missed anything?

☐ I understand my management accounts

☐ I have created my projected profit and loss

☐ I have created my cashflow forecast

My accountant is called...

My solicitor is called...

My business mentor is...

"The more you learn, the more you earn"

— *Warren Buffett*

So now you have a clear understanding of your business, what you offer, who to and why. Plus you have the financial controls in place to make sure you have a viable going concern, that you are going to manage profitably.

The next skill you need is the one that many businesses find extremely challenging and results in them being unknown. Yet when you get this right, you and your business become the go-to authority in your industry. This is the skill of **Communication**.

Now, when we talk about communication as a skill here, I mean ensuring there is a clear, concise and understandable message you and your team are communicating, which means that your clients and customers can identify the problem they are experiencing with the solution that you are providing.

This is the essence of marketing. Identify who has a problem and let them know that you have a solution for it.

Now some people believe that you have to be a marketer to do marketing or that you have to hire a marketing agency to do it all.

This can lead to lots of money spent (hundreds of thousands and more) with nothing to show for it. Ask me how I know about that! The thing is most marketeers and marketing agencies don't know your clients or customers, or your industry and especially don't know your business. So, how could they craft a clear, concise and appealing message without this?

A popular saying usually accredited to Albert Einstein is

that if he only had one hour to solve a problem, he would spend 55 minutes defining the problem and the remaining 5 minutes solving it.

Marketing is no different; you need to take the time to understand your clients or potential clients. What are their problems, their fears, their worries? What keeps them awake at night? What is stopping them from becoming a success? And only then can you start looking at how your services can help them overcome these difficulties.

There are so many businesses out there that come up with a great solution to a problem people don't have. Or a problem they do have but aren't willing to invest in resolving. The thing is, no matter how much marketing you put behind these types of solutions, you will not get any traction, no one will seek you out, and you will make no sales.

Therefore, you have to not only be seeking out the gap in the marketing so that you can carve your niche. You also need to ensure there **is** a market in the gap. Sometimes there is a valid reason for the gap that you haven't seen.

When you speak with some marketers, they will tell you that marketing is all about qualifying leads, as in identifying those people who need your product or service and communicating with them in a way that gets them to talk to you.

Qualification of leads for me is only half the truth, as marketing also needs to be a disqualification exercise. Marketing should actively repel those people and businesses that you **don't** want to do business with. For example, if you get 1000 leads through but only 1 of them has the problem now, that means you have to spend your time, or your money on your customer service/sales team is essentially providing free consultancy. Wouldn't it be better if that number was 100:1 or even better than that 10:1?

So, your communications need also to be disqualifying those who you cannot help as much as qualifying those that you can.

Consider it like trying to find that perfect gift for your significant partner or spouse, in my case, my lovely wife. Now I have options:

1) Outsource: I ask someone else to get a gift for her. They may ask a couple of questions and buy a suitable gift, but is it really personal for her? Will it really make her happy?

2) Collaborate: I work with a personal shopper or similar advisor who can tailor what I know about my wife and advise on options. This can be more expensive and takes my time as well, however, my wife is likely to get a pleasant surprise of something she would never have expected from me, and she truly enjoys.

3) Do it myself: With the knowledge I have, I then hit the shops (or at least Amazon) looking for that special something. It will be personal, and she will like it, but will probably have guessed what it was before I give it to her. And, no, it wasn't an Amazon voucher before you ask!

This is similar to finding the right 'effort mix' for your marketing. If you don't truly know what your clients need and could do some of it yourself, then don't waste money on getting a marketer to try doing it for you. You may be lucky, and they may provide something that works. The one thing you can guarantee is they will have spent your money.

ACTON: Will you spend the time to really understand the problems your clients have and how you can help them? Or are you going to just shout about your product or service and complain when you aren't getting any enquiries?

The problem I solve for my clients is … ✍

"Knowledge is the start of understanding, which is the catalyst for action. Action is the maker of greatness!"

– Martin Sharp

With this skill, you are truly serving your clients and customers to help them overcome their problem/s. Without it, you deny them an answer that only you can provide. This is the ability to **Contribute** to them positively.

Contribute in the sense of service, help and assistance. Because that is what we are trying to do, right?

There may be some snake oil salespeople or rogue traders out there who are simply trying to take other people's money for themselves. But that is not you, right?

We want our clients and customers to succeed, enjoying the products and services we provide. That way, there is a win-win scenario, in that the sum of the parts is greater than each part individually.

Also, customers who succeed themselves, whether that is from you contributing to them serving their clients or in them benefiting from what you have provided directly, will more than likely buy from you again in the future. Not only that – they will recommend you to other people, further growing your business and contributing to your success as well.

For you to be able to help them succeed there must be a win-win situation. Yet that can only happen if it is mutually beneficial, which in many cases means you will sell them a product or service. Because, like the famous analogy of the aircraft oxygen mask states, you cannot help other people unless you help yourself first.

Can you imagine simply giving away your knowledge,

services and products all the time? How long do you believe you can operate as a business with that model?

Yet there are business owners, managers and consultants I've worked with, who are doing just that because they "don't like sales" or "sales is beneath them" or "they are not salespeople".

The thing is everyone is a salesperson! Whether you are trying to deliver a project, change someone's ideas so they can overcome their problems, or help deliver your products or services. We are all in a position where we are serving the client by trying to match their problem to a solution and where we can also be the provider of that solution, doing so.

Sales isn't about trying to con someone, and I would hope that isn't you. It is a dignified and humble role that you play in trying to help someone. I'm sure your client would charge for their services and doesn't work for free all the time. Therefore, there is already a precedent set for value exchange.

The work you will have already done on your Communication skills will come in very useful with your Contribution skills. Because the information needed upfront is practically the same and the key with this skill is the specific matching of your client or customer to the specific product or service you can help them with.

I have heard the difference between Sales and Marketing described to me in military terms like the difference between artillery and a sniper. I am not saying you should be shooting your clients! Though I am sure there may be some that you'd like to fire. The problem ones. The ones that take 80% of your time and account for only 20% of your income!

However, for this analogy, the artillery is "getting the message out there" to the world, using the models that you have created based on the research you've done. This should be appealing to those who would want to work with you and draw them to you. However, would you agree you are not a model, you are an individual with your unique nuances and traits?

That is where the sniper comes in. Rather than having a conversation with your client or customer at the generic model level, you need to get to know their specific problem, how is it affecting them? What will good look like when they have overcome their problem? And from this check which of your products or services can get them to their goal. Now perhaps you can't directly help them, but you know someone who can, that you could send them to?

ACTION: Will you seek to serve your clients at the best of your ability without sacrificing yourself? Or will you simply try to sell them anything and be surprised when they complain, ask for a refund and don't help you get more business!

I provide outstanding value to my clients by ...✍

"You increase your wealth by increasing the number whom you serve."

— Martin Sharp

BEYOND THE BASIC BUSINESS

We've covered the foundational skills. Let's look at the follow on 5 skills, which when acquired and used will help propel your endeavour from the existence and survival stages of an organisation, into the stabilisation, growth, take-off and maturity phases.

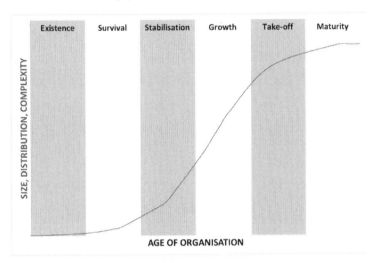

Would you agree that many of the problems you face could have been seen before and other people may have solutions for them?

With this next skill, you'll understand how to **Cultivate** your business. That is - knowing how to help it grow and capitalise on opportunities that are available.

Sometimes the fact that you don't know something could possibly be the thing that is holding you back. Look at the 4-minute mile.

Before Roger Banister smashed it in May 1954 no-one believed it was physically possible. And yet how many athletes have been able to do that, or better, since? The thing that was holding them back was the belief that it couldn't be done.

It is the same with businesses. Many of the patterns and models are cyclic. They come around again and again in different guises. If you have an understanding of them and you learn how to recognise them, then you will have at your disposal a series of proven solutions, which means you will have more confidence in being able to make the right decision at the right time.

The same goes for opportunities. Not every idea is going to be profitable. Therefore, would it be good to have a way to evaluate these and choose which ones you will pursue? It's a bit like when you make a decision to buy something, let's say a red car, do you then notice just how many red cars there are around? This is simply because they have been brought into your awareness and area of focus.

As with any muscle, you need to be training, practising and developing your skills in cultivating your business.

Some people believe these are the skills of an entrepreneur. Along with this belief are myths - like 'Entrepreneurs are born, not made'.

Yet, what I've found is that Entrepreneurship is a mindset and a skill that can be taught. People can learn to be entrepreneurial. In fact, entrepreneurial approaches to a pattern or opportunity-identification, risk management and value assessment along with being able to review how others do things and rework it for yourself are key skills that can be adapted to all areas of your business. And they can be taught to your teams.

Others believe that growth and opportunity come only out of luck or fortuitous situations, that entrepreneurs are no more than gamblers.

Luck may seem to play a part in it. Bill Gates and Steve Jobs certainly seemed to be in the right place at the right time. However, successful entrepreneurs take very careful, calculated risks and put themselves into the right places at the right time. They try to influence the odds, often getting others to share risk with them and avoiding or minimising risks if they have the choice.

Often they slice up the risk into smaller, quite digestible pieces; only then do they commit the time or resources to determine if that piece will work. They do not deliberately seek to take more risk or to take unnecessary risk, nor do they shy away from unavoidable risk.

In an interview in Golf Digest magazine in 2002, Gary Player presents an entertaining story where he was practising in a bunker down in Texas. There was a 'good old boy' with a big hat who stopped to watch. The first shot he saw Gary hit went in the hole.

He said, "You got 50 bucks if you knock the next one in." Gary holed the next one. Then he says, "You got $100 if you hole the next one." In it went - for three in a row. As he peeled off the bills, he said, "Boy, I've never seen anyone so lucky in my life." And Gary shot back, "Well, the harder I practice, the luckier I get."

ACTION: Will you learn about existing patterns for your business and how you can spot them? Will you seek out opportunities and build a method to assess which ones you'll profit from? Or will try to reinvent the wheel your way and wonder why it's taking so long to achieve your dream?

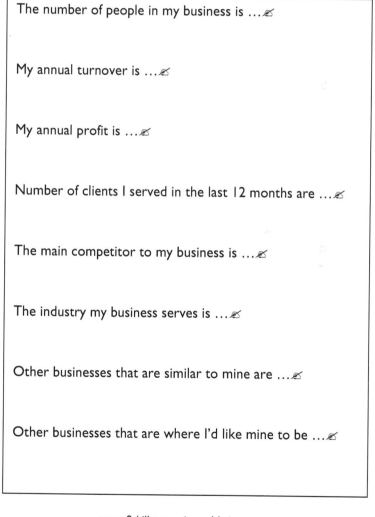

The number of people in my business is ...✍

My annual turnover is ...✍

My annual profit is ...✍

Number of clients I served in the last 12 months are ...✍

The main competitor to my business is ...✍

The industry my business serves is ...✍

Other businesses that are similar to mine are ...✍

Other businesses that are where I'd like mine to be ...✍

*"The more I can recognise, the faster
I can capitalise"* – Martin Sharp

There are many things in a business that you can direct and control. However, the culture of your business isn't one of them. That needs to be grown and comes from your changing role within the organisation and potentially your changing career. By developing your skills as being the **Chief**.

Being the Chief of your business means embracing being the leader and the manager, because your team, your vendors and your clients and customers will need someone to rally round. To know someone is there making sure they are not just doing things right, they are doing the right things.

Yet what are the right things? What should you be managing? How do you lead?

These are all great questions that you need to explore to understand what is needed by your business and in your industry.

There are many business gurus out there saying things like, "you need to be an inspirational leader, and they will follow you". For me, this is such a superficial statement, because people do follow inspirational people for a while until they realise that the actions don't match the rhetoric. Have you ever been really inspired by someone only to be disappointed not long after because their actions didn't match their words?

Now inspiration is important; it is like the spark that can ignite the fire. Yet without fuel to feed the fire, the spark won't catch and can be gone as quickly as it arrives.

There are some that state that management is red tape and dogma, which will only slow your firm down. You need to get rid of it all and embrace chaotic, flexible and agile working.

Just like food and exercise, too much of anything is bad for you and finding the right balance of processes and structure, to relationships and flexibility is probably as much an art as science. Yet there are some clear and easy ways to measure what you need to put in place to allow you to delegate and take quantifiable risks, rather than abdicate your responsibilities and take a chance it might work (or might not, red or black anyone?).

Another thing that really irritates me is the comment that leaders don't get it wrong. Surprisingly enough because everyone is human:

"Every master was once a disaster"

— T Harv Eker

If you pick up any biography from the greatest leaders in business, for example, Bill Gates, Sir Richard Branson, Felix Dennis, etc. you will read about the problems they had to overcome, some of them caused by themselves and how they overcame them to become great leaders. If this is true, then why would someone want to put such pressure on themselves to try to never make a mistake?

Being the Chief is like being the conductor of a band. You need to pull together some great and talented musicians to play a concert and be rewarded for doing so. You can decide what type of band you want to lead, one-man bad, quartet, rock group, jazz band, village brass band or symphony orchestra. Each will require you to adjust your style and cater to their needs and the needs of the audience.

As it is with your business, you can be the solopreneur, a key member of a brilliant partnership or the leader of a vast enterprise. In each of these positions, you will need to adjust your skills and approach accordingly, which will mean in many cases learning to let go of some things you currently do and embrace what and how your team needs to help you deliver your why and the why of your business.

ACTION: Are you going to concentrate on the things that need your attention and delegate those that you can? What are the processes in your business? Are you the Chief in your business and if not, what would your business look like if you were? Or will you continue to try and do everything yourself?

I spend the following percentage of time: ...✍	
Handling day-to-day operations	%
Business strategy	%
Building relationships/partnerships	%
Sales	%
HR	%
Finance/ accounting	%
Other (specify)	%
(They should add up to 100%)	

"A genuine leader is not a searcher
for consensus, but a moulder of
consensus."

— Martin Luther King Jr

Ok, it is great to talk about letting go and delegating to your team, yet how do you know that the right things are happening? How do you know that things are being done?

That is where the next skill comes into play, as when you don't have this, you'll feel out of control and fear to let go. When you use this skill, you will feel confident that you can direct and get the feedback you need to feel comfortable that the right things are happening. This is the skill to **Coordinate**.

This is the ability to build strategic growth in your business by creating, measuring and managing processes, governance, mindsets, behaviours, measures and structure.

Not everything in your business needs to be created for the first time each time. Would you agree that the first time you do something, it takes longer and can be more error-prone?

There are some people out there that advocate not putting these steps into your business. They say you should work in an agile and flexible manner relying on the expertise of those you employ and having conversations when necessary.

Can you imagine that really working in all organisations and for all tasks? What if the mechanic who replaces your brakes has never been trained and doesn't know how to do it, so goes away to work it out for themselves? Would you want to get back in that car?

Or what would happen to the taste of a Mars bar (or any other chocolate bar for that matter) if the workers made up the recipe each day? Do you think it would be consistent? Would you be able to rely on it tasting the way you remember it?

And I'd love to be there when they didn't get paid on time or the right amount because someone just did what they thought was right, as they didn't have a process.

Now don't get me wrong, there is a need to have innovative people around you, in your business and working with you because these people will help you change and grow. And at the same time, you need to know for some tasks that a process is being followed.

You may be wondering where to start?

There are many ways to do so and a variety of different methodologies you can use. However, they all boil down to some simple premises, and one place you can start is to identify what tasks are repeated in your business. Then find the person that does that task the best and write down what they do.

A word of caution though,

"Don't try to boil the ocean"

- Meg Whitman

I've seen people try to systemise everything in their business. This is very costly, especially if you haven't identified what the best method is and even more so if you try to automate it with technology.

Keep in mind the golden rule that what you are systemising must cost less or produce more (leading to more sales) than your current method.

Also, remember that while technology is great when you get it right, when you get it wrong you will only end up with a bigger and more costly problem, faster.

Systemising a business is a bit like moving to a new house, where you have two clear options. The first one is that you put everything into boxes that get loaded onto the van and transported to the destination, where you spend the next days, months (years) wondering what is in which box and complaining that you've lost something.

The other option is that you decide to group certain items, maybe by room or by use, or by colour, whatever works for you. You then set about packing the boxes. You neatly wrap or fold each item, add it to an inventory and label the box. On arriving at your destination, finding your beloved whatnots is simple as you merely refer to your system.

In this case, we can break down the house-move, putting it into different parts of the system. We have:

- ✓ A goal = To move house
- ✓ A policy = Everything is to be easily findable at the destination
- ✓ Processes = To clearly label and inventory each item, which is to be carefully wrapped and packed in a box
- ✓ Procedures = Which box for what item on what

list, wrapped which way and with what material.

ACTION: Will you seek out repetitive tasks in your business and look to systemise them, then delegate them? Or will you try to do all the work yourself?

I have the following processes for sales ...✍

I have the following processes for marketing ...✍

I have the following processes for accounting ...✍

I have the following processes for human resources ...✍

I have the following processes for operations ...✍

I have the following processes for logistics ...✍

I have the following processes for (please specify) ...✍

"Surround yourself with the best people you can find, delegate authority, and don't interfere as long as the policy you've decided upon is being carried out."

- Ronald Reagan

"Where do I find all these great people?", you may be wondering. When you get the next skill right, magic does happen, and you'll achieve the growth you were hoping for. Yet when you get it wrong, you will find the experience stressful, costly and unrewarding. You need to be able to foster your skill of building your **Community**.

This skill is all about finding, retaining and growing the right people, because with the right people in place, with delegated responsibility and the right attitude, what may once have seemed impossible becomes possible.

There are more than enough books, blog posts and studies to support the idea that hiring on attitude over skills helps you achieve more. (check out "The Book on Recruitment" by my friend Carole Fossey on Amazon which is about how to hire the 'culture match'). The thing is that with the right attitude, even when someone cannot do something because they don't have the skills, they are willing to learn. With the right attitude, they will persevere with a problem. With the right attitude, they admit their failures, learn from them and don't make them again. They have the willingness to share knowledge with others and strive for a common goal.

Then some business consultants advise you should only pay the minimum that you can get away with.

For me, that doesn't make good business sense. Put simply if someone is having money worries because you are not paying what they are worth, then their mind will not be focused on the tasks at hand. You won't get their best. They'll probably resent you and probably be looking for another job. I mean, would you stick at the same job if you thought you were worth more?

And that's before we start looking at the financial cost of having to find someone, train them, and the disruption in your business while that happens. The disruption to your team as they go through the Forming – Storming - Norming – Performing cycle, all of these impact your growth, profitability and sustainability.

Some people are quite worried about employing people, especially in the early stages of their business. With all the responsibility of someone else's livelihood, the regulations and bureaucracy required by governments and the law, I can understand why.

Yet there are ways to make it easier for yourself and to de-risk elements. One way is to use other small businesses or independent freelancers. If you do hire someone, there are HR agencies set up to help. In fact, some accountants and solicitors offer these services, and you've already got them in place as part of your foundational four, right?

So, you can think about building your community in a similar way to investing money. When you are investing money, you are looking for an opportunity to gain a return on your investment either in the form of interest payment, a dividend or profit from a sale. In some cases, you may even borrow someone else's money, such as leveraging the bank's money for the mortgage on a property or leveraging a business angel's money to build and grow a business.

You'll do this by understanding what the investment is,

how it works and taking the acceptable amount of risk in order to seize the opportunity and make it work.

The same goes for the community you will grow. Here you are looking to support your business growth, profitability and sustainability by leveraging other people's expertise, knowledge and time in exchange for a reward, usually in the form of remuneration of some kind.

Just like any investment, you should be looking to understand what value they will bring to the business, how you will see a return on your investment in them and take the appropriate risk that you can manage in order to move your business forward.

ACTION: How will you build the community in your business to allow it to grow? Or are you simply hoping you don't end up with a "bad investment" by bringing on board the wrong people.

I will find the right people to help serve my clients by ... ✍

"Hire on attitude, train for skill"

— Harvard Business Review

 Once you have started to build your team, then you need to be exercising the last skill. Without this skill, you will find that you become uncomfortable in your business and when you develop this skill you will find everyone that is part of your business behaves in a way that supports your business concept. That is the skill of directing **Conduct**.

When you are a solopreneur or a very small business, you will find that your values and ethics are closely tied to the success of the business, along with being clearly understood by those around you.

However, this close community becomes more diluted the more people that are involved. The result is that the values and ethics that are the foundation of the business also become diluted and could directly affect the growth, profitability and sustainability of your business, costing you money, time and credibility.

The good news is there are ways that can help you develop a great company culture that will support your business achieve the concept that you envisaged.

Some people will tell you that company culture cannot be imposed, it must be nurtured, and you cannot create it yourself.

This is a partial truth, as the culture is the way your business lives and breathes, it is about values and behaviour. Just like a plant, you can and do affect the culture by feeding and caring for it, giving it enough light and considering every component of the system. Influencers at all levels need to work together.

While culture does say a lot about 'how things are done around here' it has to be grown from the collective hearts and habits of everyone working in the business. Company culture requires a movement, not a mandate. Just like a plant, if you don't feed it or care for it or you feed it the wrong food, then the plant will wither and potentially attract nasty things like an infestation of aphids or an outbreak of mould or fungus. Or in business terms, a poor company culture could result in poor working practices, poor cost control and lack of accountability.

There isn't a quick fix to getting this right, as it's not about things. Bean bags and foosball tables may be great perks, but they are not the culture.

I've seen some people focus solely on the good of the business, with the belief that, that is after all, why everyone is there. Yet, would you agree, that this is incredibly short-sighted? The needs of each person involved also matter because their reason for doing what they do, is probably not the same as your reason? And if everyone's needs aren't met, their negative feelings will start to degrade your culture.

Culture change or improvement doesn't have to be extravagant or expensive to implement. One of the effective ways is to make sure the people in the business feel valued and have a role to play.

Have you noticed how people seem to flock to businesses that have a great culture, and how these companies seem to be able to retain staff? This is not just about staff, though, as a great culture will make clients and vendors want to continue to do business with them because they feel valued too.

Go back in your mind to your favourite restaurant. Picture being there. What does it sound like? What does it look like? What does it smell like? Are you sitting at your favourite table? Does the waiter know what you like or is he suggesting something delightful from the menu? Who are you sharing this experience with?

Now compare that feeling you have when picking up a pre-packaged sandwich from the shop or garage.

Which would you prefer? That experience is culture.

ACTION: Are you going to take positive actions to grow a positive culture? Are you going to put things in place to help foster that growth like soil and light helps a plant to grow? Or are you going to deal with whatever the consequences are, even if it costs you your company?

I will influence the culture in my company by ...✍

"Your beliefs become your thoughts,

Your thoughts become your words,

Your words become your actions,

Your actions become your habits,

Your habits become your values,

Your values become your destiny."

— Gandhi

WHAT BUSINESS DO YOU ASPIRE

TO GROW?

Whether you study academic texts like the Portable MBA series, industry journals like the Harvard Business Review or industry case studies and business growth programmes from Goldman Sachs, PWC, KPMG and others or blog articles from across the internet, one thing they all have in common is that businesses grow in phases.

Each growth phase has its challenges and characteristics. As the entrepreneurs and business owners, you have a choice as to what business you aspire to.

"Start with the end in mind" –
Stephen Covey

If you understand what you aspire to, your end goal for your business, from there you can work out what you need to do and learn. And you will learn what phases you will need to transition through to get there. Maybe you have your heart set on building a multi-million-pound (or billion perhaps) business and going for a public sale. Or perhaps you are building a business for a private sale. Potentially you are looking to build a family business to provide a legacy.

You may be thinking, "I don't want to have a big business. I'm happy to build a growing, profitable and sustainable small business" and this is fine. The thing is, it is your choice, and there are many examples of great businesses that choose not to grow big. In the book, "Small Giants: Companies That Choose to Be Great Instead of Big", by Bo Burlingham, he provides case studies of maverick companies that passed up the growth treadmill and focused on greatness instead.

Let's have a look at 6 business models and how they relate to the UK business market as it is in 2019. Because if you understand the characteristics of these businesses, then you can see which is most similar to your own and look at some of the known success factors, growth challenges, key crisis and opportunities along with which skills you should be focused on.

As with all models, there are exceptions, and if you are one of them, congratulations again. Models, by their nature should be a simplistic representation of real things. Otherwise, with all the many permutations around, a model will cease to have any meaning. A bit like humans are part of the tree of life and can be described along the branches from life to animals to mammals to apes to man. That doesn't specifically describe you or me, but it is good enough to start looking for patterns and characteristics.

You may be wondering, "Will all businesses suffer the crises mentioned? Will I need to stick rigidly to the growth patterns and seek success only as described?"

The short answer is no. Some businesses may adapt without suffering any obvious panics or crises. This could be because of luck, or because the owner is already aware these are coming and has put in place the appropriate actionable plans at the right times.

And if you think that external political, social, technological, legal or environmental factors may have a direct effect on growth and opportunities, that is not illustrated in the model; you are also correct. As with any prediction of the future, it is not a fact until it is time.

"In theory, there is no difference
between theory and practice. In
practice, there is." - Albert Einstein

SOLOPRENEUR / SOLE PROPRIETOR

The term Solopreneur is defined by the Oxford English Dictionary as, "..a person who sets up and runs a business on their own". They represent the largest number of businesses in the UK at circa 4 million, according to the UK Government Office for National Statistics at the time of first publication. These businesses may or may not employ people and are maybe VAT registered if they exceed the current threshold of £86,000.

Typically, a solopreneur works on their own or employs perhaps one other person. They may use external service providers such as accountants, solicitors, personal assistants, web developers and so on to supplement and support their effort. Therefore, it could be argued, that they support more people (full-time equivalent employees) with the business they generate and fulfil.

The average revenue in this category is £64,000. However, there is a large fluctuation in the skills and rates for those in this model, including coaches, consultants, trades, independent contractors and cottage businesses to mention a few.

Most early-stage micro-businesses start here with potential for growth and share many of the success factors, growth challenges and opportunities characteristics of the solopreneur.

As the typical "Chef, cook and bottle washer" business, the solopreneur must handle all aspects of the business. Success in this model is not just in the skills of the craft employed, albeit having a high quality and desirable product or service does help. They must be masters of time management and salesmanship to ensure everything is dealt with and a revenue stream is forthcoming.

As a highly flexible business model, they can pivot and change direction quickly to take advantage of the current opportunities, whether they are political, social, technological, legal or environmental. They grow through creativity and adaption.

Although not everything is perfect with many sufferings a crisis of leadership, crashing between feast & famine with no real planning and a sense of panic over when the next opportunity to will arise. This leads to poor choices, snapping up anything that will potentially pay or being distracted by shiny penny syndrome, at the cost of their time, additional equipment, additional training and so on, even impacting their health and that of their families.

It is essential at this stage that the skills of Concept, Control, Communication & Contribution.

MICRO BUSINESS

You've got a few employees, well at least the two of you and less than double figures and you have an idea that is working. Congratulations! You find yourself at the micro-business level. There are over a million businesses in the UK that operate in this model employing over 4 million people and turning over nearly half a million pounds on average per year.

The micro business now has a lot more responsibilities with forecasting and planning becoming more critical to ensure that the business continues to operate as a going concern.

Still a highly flexible business model, they can pivot and change direction quickly to take advantage of the current opportunities, whether they are political, social, technological, legal or environmental. Although now they grow through strong leadership and good direction.

Success more likely hinges on alignment to a singular vision, the development and execution of a great marketing strategy and delivery of a quality service unrivalled in its market space.

One of the key problems here is a crisis of autonomy. That is letting others get on with what is needed without the directional control or micromanagement. The owner/founder/leader struggles with letting go as the business is getting too big for the leader to get involved in everything. Informal communication structure starts to fail, and a modicum of functional management structure is required.

Alongside the mastering the skills of Concept, Control, Communication & Contribution, you must also start mastering your skills of Cultivation, embracing your changing role as the Chief and empowering through Coordination. It is worthwhile starting to exercise your skills in building your community and instilling the right conduct. Getting these rights now, could save you major headaches later.

SMALL BUSINESS

If you've reached the small business mark, well done. It is not an easy journey, and you've probably had your fair share of early mornings and late nights. Yet, if you've been developing the skills you needed to be a Microbusiness, then you have in place many of the key pieces you'll need to continue to grow as a small business.

In the UK, there are over two hundred thousand small businesses with average annuals sales of £2.8 million and employing up to 50 people.

At this stage, there is a major decision to be made that will impact your growth. Do you seek to disengage from growing the business, become a "Small Giant" and continue to run as the steady operation you've built, continuing in seeking excellence at the level you've achieved? Or do you go for growth, perhaps with a private sale exit in mind or a public share offering?

The key crisis you are looking to get over is one of control. For either option to work, you will need to start putting in a more formal management structure and then grow through delegation.

This will mean alongside the mastery you are developing in your skills of Concept, Control, Communication, Contribution, Cultivation, Chief and Coordination, you must also now be mastering your ability to build a community and ensure the right Conduct is followed.

So, if you chose the path of excellence and your aim is to be a "Small Giant", then you will need to be making a more functional hires to ensure success. These will be people who take over certain duties performed by the owner and have operational responsibilities as part of the function delegation.

If you are going for growth, then you will need to make more strategic hires and probably understand that for many you will pay a lot more than you anticipated and this will be money well spent. With strategic hires, you are not only looking for functional responsibility; you are also looking for their contribution to strategic growth.

MEDIUM BUSINESS

You went for growth and through some strategic hires have grown your business to somewhere between 50 and 250 people. Your business is one of over 35,000 in the UK that supports an average revenue of over £17 million.

At this stage, a lot of your success will come down to strategic planning and execution of the plan. The delegated responsibility and accountability that you have placed in the strategic hires will continue to push the business forward as they also strive for growth. This will come through coordination and collaboration between departments and also with outside partners.

However, there is an underbelly that may be growing, stifling profits in the form of bureaucracy, red tape and slow decision making. This could be in the form of people dodging decisions because they don't want to responsible for it or could be that as the processes have grown some are no longer required or exist only to perpetuate themselves, a cottage industry within your organisation. If action isn't taken to identify these and eradicate them, them, then your business will miss external opportunities and be slow to the market.

You are no longer a nimble micro or small business.

You need to continue to master the skills of Concept, Control, Communication, Contribution, Cultivation, Chief, Coordination, Community and Conduct and run a great operation. And you also need to build your skills in Scaling a business and managing continuous transformation.

LARGE BUSINESS

If you aspired to own a large business, then you will certainly have mastered the skills Concept, Control, Communication, Contribution, Cultivation, Chief, Coordination, Community and Conduct and run a great operation. You need to build your skills in Scaling a business and managing continuous transformation.

Although at this point you will have other people who are expert in their respective areas. Perhaps a Human Resources Director, a Chief Finance Officer, a Chief Operations Officer, an Enterprise Architect, and so on. The skills you have mastered will help you in understanding the responses to your strategic direction.

The further success of your business is now based on leadership development and ensuring your senior management team and all levels of management along with all those who are part of your business are developing the skills not only in their area of expertise, but also in the building and running of a successful business. Because each project, department and initiative will go through similar problems to building and growing a small business.

You may suffer a crisis of innovation, especially if there is slow decision making and red tape, potentially leading to creating small "skunkworks" operations to provide the agility you need as the main business runs out of ideas.

Growth is more likely to come through strategic alliances or acquisition.

Therefore, growing your skills in assessing businesses, corporate negotiation and innovation at scale should be paramount.

...✍	My business is a...	I aspire to be...
Solopreneur		
Micro Business		
Small Business		
Medium Business		
Large Business		

	Lifestyle		Disengage
SHARP ASTUTE CONSULTING	Solopreneur/ Sole Proprietors	Micro Business	Small Business Steady Operation - Disengagement
# of Employees	1	2-9	10-49
Annual Sales	£64,000	£468,000	£2,800,000
# in UK	4,278,000 (75%)	1,138,000 (20.07%)	210,000 (3.7%)
Success Factor	Time & Salesmanship	Marketing, Service & Vision	Functional Hires
Grow Through	Creativity	Direction	Delegation
Crisis of	Leadership	Autonomy	Control
Skills	CONCEPT CONTROL COMMUNICATION CONTRIBUTION	As Solopreneaur Plus: CULTIVATION CHIEF COORDINATION	As Micro Business Plus: COMMUNITY CONDUCT

Growing Service in a niche community.

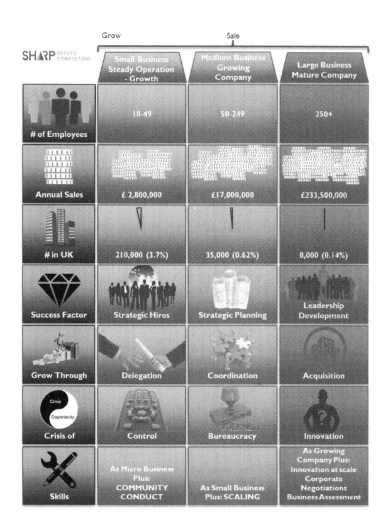

	Grow	Sale	
SHARP ASTUTE CONSULTING	**Small Business** Steady Operation - Growth	**Medium Business** Growing Company	**Large Business** Mature Company
# of Employees	10-49	50-249	250+
Annual Sales	£ 2,800,000	£17,000,000	£233,500,000
# in UK	210,000 (3.7%)	35,000 (0.62%)	8,000 (0.14%)
Success Factor	Strategic Hires	Strategic Planning	Leadership Development
Grow Through	Delegation	Coordination	Acquisition
Crisis of	Control	Bureaucracy	Innovation
Skills	As Micro Business Plus: COMMUNITY CONDUCT	As Small Business Plus: SCALING	As Growing Company Plus: Innovation at scale Corporate Negotiations Business Assessment

Growing for scale and sale.

*"The future belongs to those who
believe in the beauty of their dreams."*

- Eleanor Roosevelt

WHAT HAPPENS NOW?

In the previous chapters we have covered the 9 skills necessary to ensure you survive and thrive in business. Here's the thing, just reading about them won't bring the results, you need to put action behind each one.

If you are starting with the *Foundational Four*, looking at the importance of knowing and sharing your **Concept**. To make sure you have a clear understanding of what and why YOU are doing this? What will YOU get from it? What sacrifices are YOU willing to make it work? And that you have communicated these clearly.

Did you write down your business concept and did you share it with those in your business?

With the skill of **Control,** we explored some of the financial management tasks you need to be involved in and the importance of planning and measuring against these to ensure you know where you are and where you are going.

Have you reviewed the 3 financial statements of your firm and have you asked questions, so you understand what they are telling you?

In **Communication** and **Contribution,** the importance of knowing your customers was touched on. As was getting the right message out to help qualify those you can help and disqualify those you can't. This helps you in being able to use your time wisely to serve more.

Have you spent time to really understand the problems your clients have and how you can help to solve them?

In *Beyond the Basic Business,* we examined the 5 skills needed to build a business beyond survival through stabilisation to growth, take-off and maturity. This started with working on your **Cultivation** skills for your business. That way, you can take advantage of those who have built businesses before you to recognise and capitalise on more opportunities that come your way.

Do you know about the existing patterns in business, how you can spot them and what you can do with that knowledge to improve your business?

Then we looked at your changing role in the business as you improve your skills as the **Chief** and move from working solely in your business, to working on your business.

Are you concentrating on the things that need your attention and delegating everything that you can?

Building strategic growth in your business through systemisation by developing your **Coordination** skills, we explored how to ensure you focus on the right high ticket tasks and have a method to delegate and not abdicate your responsibilities. With the outcome being a predictable, reliable and consistent experience for your clients, vendors and those in your business.

Have you identified all the repetitive tasks in your business and systemised them?

The importance of you building your skill of **Community** was outlined to ensure you get the right people to do the right thing at the right time.

Have you identified who you need in your community to allow your business to grow?

Finally, the skill of **Conduct** to ensure you create a business culture that attracts great talent and great clients.

Have you taken positive actions to grow a positive culture?

Would you agree, that to improve your chances of success you need to take action? And to increase the chances of you following through on those actions and commitments, it is best to write them down? The act of writing them down gets you to remember them by using not just your mind. It uses the motor memory of the action of writing and the motivational element that if it is written down, others may see it and hold you to account.

So, pick up your pen or your laptop and write down your answers to each of the action questions as your commitment to your business growth, profitability and sustainability and to yourself. Review it often and seek out more ways to improve your business.

*"Growth equals change. If you want to
get better, you have to keep changing
and improving. That means stepping
out into new areas."* - John Maxwell

If you have found this information valuable and are looking for more information on how you can improve your skills so you can build a growing, profitable and sustainable business, then you can get access to free resources here:

Find more great resources to help push you further forward by visiting
✓ www.9skillstosurviveandthrive.com

Also, get your questions answered and join in the conversation on our Facebook group
✓ facebook.com/groups/GrowthProfitabilitySustaina bility/

ABOUT THE AUTHOR

WHY I WROTE THIS BOOK

After running successful businesses for over 10 years and helping others to grow profitable and sustainable businesses, I wanted to share what I had learned about the key skills necessary in running such a business. These are the traits that I have found successfully drive businesses forward to greater success and improve the lives of those working in them. And I realised that writing a book was perhaps a great option.

Having worked across a wide range of sectors from Pharmaceuticals, Aerospace companies, Universities, Councils, Motor and Drinks manufacturers, Airport operators, hospitals through to countless smaller businesses, these 9 skills I've identified come up time and again in all my successes and the successes of my clients.

"Another masterpiece session with Mr Sharp. We can't speak highly enough about the level he is putting his mentoring classes and dedication to detail. Thank you for an amazing session and valuable feedback, which helps us to grow. It's an honour to be able to get through this amazing journey with you."

- Norik Koczarian

MARTIN SHARP

An International Business Transformer; Award-Winning, Speaker & Trainer; And the bestselling author of the award-winning book Digital Transformation. Delivering Successful Change in Business Environments.

Martin can give you, as the leader, owner, entrepreneur, manager or empowered change agent, power and confidence in maximising the potential of your business.

If you have ever given up on something technically complicated or felt that there must 'be an easier way', then you need to talk to Martin and hear him speak. He consistently brings clarity to the most complex issues. Navigating the complicated and ever-changing landscape, Martin's pragmatic solutions deliver change and realise business benefit within every organisation, every time.

Martin Sharp has worked in the corporate and entrepreneurial world since 1993 and in his own consulting firm since 2009, delivering transformational change to clients across a wide range of sectors from Pharmaceuticals, Aerospace companies, Universities, Councils, Motor and Drinks manufacturers, Airport operators and hospitals through to countless small businesses.

Clients have described Martin as "Knowledgeable, personable, refreshing, unbiased, diligent, help!" and "A breath of fresh air in a world where complexity often seems to create as many challenges as it solves."

He is an enthusiastic leader, helping companies to

structure their technology, removing the barriers so that technology becomes a business enabler, empowering communication & growth.

Helping you build growing, profitable and sustainable businesses.

Web	www.martinsharp.com
Facebook	fb.me/martinsharpuk
Linkedin	uk.linkedin.com/in/martinsharp
YouTube	youtube.com/martinsharpgb

REFERENCES

Publication

Small Business Britain	https://www.goldmansachs.com/citiz enship/10000-small-businesses/UK/news-and-events/building-business-britain-f/report.pdf
UK Gov. Office for National Statistics, Business births, deaths and survival rates	https://www.ons.gov.uk/businessind ustryandtrade/changestobusiness/bu sinessbirthsdeathsandsurvivalrates
UK SIC 2007 The current Standard Industrial Classification (SIC) used in classifying business establishments and other statistical units by the type of economic activity in which they are engaged.	https://www.ons.gov.uk/methodolog y/classificationsandstandards/ukstan dardindustrialclassificationofeconom icactivities/uksic2007
Department for Business, Energy & Industrial Strategy: Business population estimates for the UK and regions 2017	https://assets.publishing.service.gov. uk/government/uploads/system/uplo ads/attachment_data/file/663235/bp e_2017_statistical_release.pdf
House of Commons Library: Business Statistics	https://researchbriefings.files.parliam ent.uk/documents/SN06152/SN061 52.pdf
The top 9 reasons small businesses fail	https://www.hiscox.co.uk/business-blog/top-9-reasons-small-businesses-fail/

A report on growing micro businesses - Lord Young, May 2013

https://assets.publishing.service.gov.uk/government/uploads/system/uploads/attachment_data/file/198165/growing-your-business-lord-young.pdf

Department for Business Innovation 7 Skills: Research into Mid-Size Business Growth

https://assets.publishing.service.gov.uk/government/uploads/system/uploads/attachment_data/file/16422/11-1409-research-mid-size-business-growth.pdf

The Five Stages of Small Business Growth

https://hbr.org/1983/05/the-five-stages-of-small-business-growth

THE STATE OF SMALL BUSINESS: Putting UK entrepreneurs on the map

http://stateofsmallbiz.com/downloads/the-state-of-small-business.pdf

BEAT THE STATISTICS

Are you looking to build a growing, profitable and sustainable business? Amazon Bestselling author and creator of the Growing Business Generator Martin Sharp takes you through the foundational 4 key skills that he has developed, beyond his technical expertise, that has provided success time and again in building his own, growing, profitable and sustainable businesses since 2009 and over 20 years delivering successful transformational change in other peoples companies.

Beat The Statistics : The 9 skills to ensure you survive and thrive in business includes topics such as:

* What the UK business landscape is today and how to prosper in it.
* How you can align those around you fulfil your business aspiration.
* How to predict what will happens with your business.
* A greater ability to make sure your message hits home every time.
* Improve your success in winning new business.

"Martin is a consummate professional with a deep technical understanding. Good on detail and able to identify and articulate sound solutions. I would highly recommend Martin."
- **Andrew George, Programme and Delivery at NATS**

"Another great session with Martin Sharp done!!! We feel that each time he challenges us to be better and better which is exactly what we need. We look forward to implement Martins advice."
- **Norik Koczarian, Co-Founder of MN Mastery and NK Performance**

About the author

Having worked across a wide range of sectors including Pharmaceuticals, Aerospace companies, Universities, Councils, Motor and Drinks manufacturers, Airport operators, hospitals through to countless smaller businesses, he has identified these 9 skills come up time and again in all his successes and the successes of his clients.

Join Martin as he uncomplicates the complicated and shares with you simple steps to growing your business, grow your profitability and do this with sustainability.

The price of GBP £14.99; USD $19.97;
AUS $19.97; CAN $24.00; EURO €19.00

ASTUTE
BUSINESSES

47252338R00063

Printed in Poland
by Amazon Fulfillment
Poland Sp. z o.o., Wrocław